THE OFFICIAL
LEEDS UNITED
ANNUAL 2019

Written by Jordan Owens

Designed by Jon Dalrymple

A Grange Publication

© 2018. Published by Grange Communications Ltd., Edinburgh, under licence from Leeds United Football Club. Printed in the EU.

Photographs © Varley Picture Agency / Yorkshire Evening Post

ISBN 978-1-912595-11-2

C000285962

WELCOME TO THE OFFICIAL LEEDS UNITED ANNUAL 2019

As we head into 2019, everyone is hoping this can be the year Leeds United return to the Premier League.

The 2017/18 campaign was a season which had many ups and downs. There was a fine run at the start, but it ultimately ended short of expectations. However, there is now renewed hope once again at Elland Road.

In this year's annual, we take a look at the squad who are tasked with trying to guide the Whites back to the top flight.

We also welcome Marcelo Bielsa to Leeds United and look into his background, philosophies and his achievements in the game to date.

You can get to know the Leeds United players even more and test your knowledge on the club with a series of quizzes and puzzles to challenge even the most devoted fan!

We hope you enjoy it.

Marching on Together!

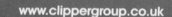

www.clippergroup.co.uk

CONTENTS

SEASON REVIEW 2017-18

AUGUST

Sunday 6th August
Sky Bet Championship
Bolton Wanderers 2
(Madine 39, Le Fondre pen 67)
Leeds United 3
(Phillips 7, 42, Wood 30)
Venue: Macron Stadium
Attendance: 19,857

Wednesday 9th August
Carabao Cup Round 1
Leeds United 4
(Saíz 12, 60, 62, Ekuban 83)
Port Vale 1
(Tonge 37)
Venue: Elland Road
Attendance: 15,431

Saturday 12th August
Sky Bet Championship
Leeds United 0
Preston North End 0
Venue: Elland Road
Attendance: 32,880

Tuesday 15th August
Sky Bet Championship
Leeds United 0
Fulham 0
Venue: Elland Road
Attendance: 28,918

Saturday 19th August
Sky Bet Championship
Sunderland 0
Leeds United 2
(Saíz 21, Dallas 76)
Venue: Stadium of Light
Attendance: 31,237

Tuesday 22nd August
Carabao Cup Round 2
Leeds United 5
(Roofe 44, 49, 65, Saíz 78, Vieira 89)
Newport County 1
(Labadie 33)
Venue: Elland Road
Attendance: 17,098

Saturday 26th August
Sky Bet Championship
Nottingham Forest 0
Leeds United 2
(Roofe 24, Alioski 87)
Venue: City Ground
Attendance: 25,682

Highlight: Nottingham Forest 0-2 Leeds United
Leeds United ended the opening month of the campaign with a dominant performance at the City Ground to keep up their unbeaten start to the season, with a two goal victory against Nottingham Forest. Kemar Roofe headed home from close range in the first half to give Leeds the lead, before troublesome winger Ezgjan Alioski doubled the lead three minutes from time, he picked the ball up outside of the box, before delivering a beautiful strike into the bottom corner.

Lowlight: Leeds United 0-0 Preston North End
With the Whites starting the season unbeaten and keeping four clean sheets in the Sky Bet Championship in the month of August, picking out a lowlight is difficult. In the 0-0 draw against Preston North End at Elland Road, Ben Pearson saw red for the visitors and Leeds had several opportunities to win the game, but were left to rue missed chances in front of goal, as both sides had to settle for a point.

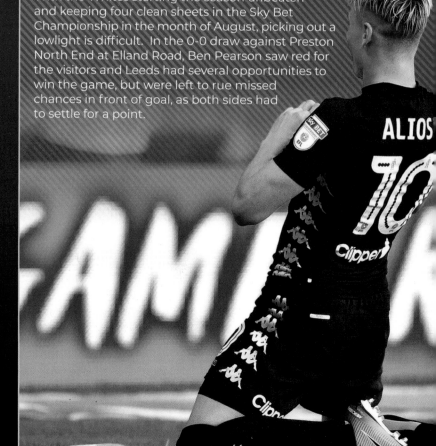

SEPTEMBER

Saturday 9th September
Sky Bet Championship
Leeds United 5
(Lasogga 20, 59, Phillips 35,
Hernández pen 44, Roofe 54)
Burton Albion 0
Venue: Elland Road
Attendance: 33,404

Tuesday 12th September
Sky Bet Championship
Leeds United 2
(Saíz 17, Dallas 90+2)
Birmingham City 0
Venue: Elland Road
Attendance: 31,507

Saturday 16th September
Sky Bet Championship
Millwall 1
(O'Brien 73)
Leeds United 0
Venue: The Den
Attendance: 16,447

Tuesday 19th September
Carabao Cup Round 3
Burnley 2
(Wood pen 89, Brady 90+6)
Leeds 2
(Sacko 80, Hernandez pen 90+4)
Leeds win 5-3 on penalties
Venue: Turf Moor
Attendance: 11,799

Saturday 23rd September
Sky Bet Championship
Leeds United 3
(Lasogga 13, Phillips 32,
Bialkowski O.G 67)
Ipswich Town 2
(McGoldrick 30, Garner 71)
Venue: Elland Road
Attendance: 34,002

Tuesday 26th September
Sky Bet Championship
Cardiff City 3
(Zohore 28, 59, Hoilett 37)
Leeds United 1
(Roofe 67)
Venue: Cardiff City Stadium
Attendance: 27,160

Highlight: Leeds United 5-0 Burton Albion
Leeds recorded a rampant 5-0 victory over Burton Albion at Elland Road as the Whites extended their unbeaten run to eight matches in all competitions. Debutant striker Pierre-Michel Lasogga hit a brace in the match after joining the club on a season-long loan from Hamburg on transfer deadline day. Pablo Hernández scored a penalty and Kalvin Phillips and Kemar Roofe sealed what would turn out to be the biggest victory of the season.

Lowlight: Millwall 1-0 Leeds United
The Whites suffered a first defeat of the season as Millwall secured three points at The Den. Former Leeds striker Steve Morison saw an early effort ruled out for offside, but the crucial blow came in the 73rd minute when Aiden O'Brien was found in space in the Leeds box and he slotted home. The result meant that Leeds had lost eight of their last nine meetings against Millwall at The Den.

OCTOBER

Sunday 1st October
Sky Bet Championship
Sheffield Wednesday 3
(Hooper 25, 41, Lee 82)
Leeds United 0
Venue: Hillsborough
Attendance: 27,972

Saturday 14th October
Sky Bet Championship
Leeds United 0
Reading 1
(Barrow 84)
Venue: Elland Road
Attendance: 33,900

Saturday 21st October
Sky Bet Championship
Bristol City 0
Leeds United 3
(Saíz 4, 14, Lasogga 67)
Venue: Ashton Gate
Attendance: 24,435

Tuesday 24th October
Carabao Cup Round 4
Leicester City 3
(Iheanacho 30, Slimani 71, Mahrez 88)
Leeds United 1
(Hernández 26)
Venue: King Power Stadium
Attendance: 31,516

Friday 27th October
Sky Bet Championship
Leeds United 1
(Phillips 34)
Sheffield United 2
(Sharp 2, Brooks 81)
Venue: Elland Road
Attendance: 34,504

Tuesday 31st October
Sky Bet Championship
Leeds United 1
(Lasogga 7)
Derby County 2
(Winnall 72, pen 80)
Venue: Elland Road
Attendance: 28,565

Highlight: Bristol City 0-3 Leeds United
Leeds got back to winning ways in emphatic style, with a fine 3-0 victory over Bristol City at Ashton Gate. An early Samuel Saíz brace gave Leeds a 2-0 lead against the Robins, who were previously unbeaten at home. After the break, Pierre-Michel Lasogga found the net with a bullet header following a Kalvin Phillips corner. Both sides were reduced to 10 men late on, with Gaetano Berardi and Matty Taylor sent off. The result proved to be United's biggest away win of the season.

Lowlight: Sheffield Wednesday 3-0 Leeds United
Leeds suffered a third successive away defeat as Sheffield Wednesday ran out 3-0 winners at Hillsborough. Leeds started the game brightly with Samuel Saíz causing problems, but two Gary Hooper headers saw the home side go into the break with a 2-0 advantage. Pierre-Michel Lasogga and Barry Bannan hit the woodwork for both sides, before Kieran Lee smashed home a third, to secure the Owls the points and victory in the Yorkshire derby.

NOVEMBER

Saturday 4th November
Sky Bet Championship
Brentford 3
(Maupay 22, Barbet 85, Woods 90+3)
Leeds United 1
(Alioski 67)
Venue: Griffin Park
Attendance: 11,068

Sunday 19th November
Sky Bet Championship
Leeds United 2
(Hernández 24, Alioski 54)
Middlesbrough 1
(Assombalonga pen 77)
Venue: Elland Road
Attendance: 33,771

Wednesday 22nd November
Sky Bet Championship
Wolverhampton Wanderers 4
(Douglas 15, Cavaleiro 26, Jota 72, Costa pen 76)
Leeds United 1
(Alioski 48)
Venue: Molineux
Attendance: 28,914

Saturday 25th November
Sky Bet Championship
Barnsley 0
Leeds United 2
(Saíz 23, Alioski 45+4)
Venue: Oakwell
Attendance: 16,399

Highlight: Leeds United 2-1 Middlesbrough
There was a lot riding on Middlesbrough's visit to Elland Road in November. Leeds came into the match on the back of four straight losses, whilst former Whites head coach Garry Monk returned after resigning in the close season before becoming Boro boss. It was Leeds who came out on top though, thanks to a goal in each half from Pablo Hernández and Ezgjan Alioski. Britt Assombalonga's penalty proved to be a consolation for the visitors.

Lowlight: Brentford 3-1 Leeds United
Leeds suffered a fourth defeat in succession as Brentford ran out 3-1 winners at Griffin Park. Brentford went ahead when goalkeeper Andy Lonergan spilt a cross and Neal Maupay headed home. Leeds got level in the second half when Daniel Bentley dropped a cross and Ezgjan Alioski headed in, but the Bees side came away with the win though after Yoann Barbet's low free-kick found the bottom corner and Ryan Woods smashed home a third in injury time.

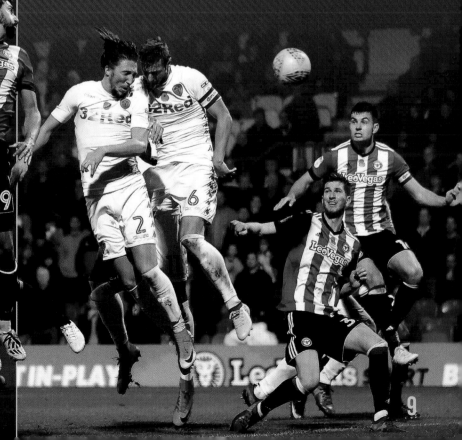

DECEMBER

Friday 1st December
Sky Bet Championship
Leeds United 1
(Jansson 19)
Aston Villa 1
(Lansbury 71)
Venue: Elland Road
Attendance: 30,547

Saturday 9th December
Sky Bet Championship
Queens Park Rangers 1
(Wszolek 90)
Leeds United 3
(Roofe 63, 68, 90+4)
Venue: Loftus Road
Attendance: 15,506

Saturday 16th December
Sky Bet Championship
Leeds United 1
(Jansson 41)
Norwich City 0
Venue: Elland Road
Attendance: 30,590

Saturday 23rd December
Sky Bet Championship
Leeds United 1
(Hernández 29)
Hull City 0
Venue: Elland Road
Attendance: 35,156

Tuesday 26th December
Sky Bet Championship
Burton Albion 1
(Naylor 29)
Leeds United 2
(Hernández 61, Roofe 64)
Venue: Pirelli Stadium
Attendance: 5,612

Saturday 30th December
Sky Bet Championship
Birmingham City 1
(Maghoma 83)
Leeds United 0
Venue: St Andrew's
Attendance: 21,673

Highlight: Queens Park Rangers 1-3 Leeds United
Kemar Roofe scored a superb second half hat-trick to secure Leeds a fine 3-1 victory over Queens Park Rangers in early December. Roofe superbly leapt highest to head home Ezgjan Alioski's cross in the 63rd minute, before doubling the lead five minutes later, converting a neat low cross from substitute Pawel Cibicki. Pawel Wszolek pulled a goal back, but Leeds sealed the win in stoppage time, when Roofe was played into the box and he fired home.

Lowlight: Birmingham City 1-0 Leeds United
The Whites went to St Andrew's in great form, undefeated in six matches, having won five of those. However, the Whites succumbed to the Blues, who sat at the bottom of the table at the time. Pablo Hernández hit the crossbar for Leeds, but Birmingham got the winner late on, when Felix Wiedwald could only parry Jota's shot into the path of Jacques Maghoma, who slotted home, to ensure a miserable end to 2017.

JANUARY

Monday 1st January
Sky Bet Championship
Leeds United 0
Nottingham Forest 0
Venue: Elland Road
Attendance: 32,426

Sunday 7th January
Emirates FA Cup Third Round
Newport County 2
(Shaughnessy OG 76, McClousky 89)
Leeds United 1
(Berardi 9)
Venue: Rodney Parade
Attendance: 6,887

Saturday 13th January
Sky Bet Championship
Ipswich Town 1
(Celina 67)
Leeds United 0
Venue: Portman Road
Attendance: 18,638

Saturday 20th January
Sky Bet Championship
Leeds United 3
(Lasogga 46, 62, Roofe 55)
Millwall 4
(O'Brien 18, Gregory 42, Elliott 87, Wallace 90+2)
Venue: Elland Road
Attendance: 33,564

Tuesday 30th January
Sky Bet Championship
Hull City 0
Leeds United 0
Venue: KCOM Stadium
Attendance: 17,237

Highlight: Hull City 0-0 Leeds United
The Whites arrested a run of three straight defeats by picking up a decent point and and a clean sheet on the road against Hull City at the KCOM Stadium. Samuel Saíz, Eunan O'Kane and Liam Cooper were all sent off in each of the previous three matches, so United had a depleted squad for the short trip to the East Coast. Both sides had chances to win the game, but neither side could beat Felix Wiedwald or Allan McGregor between the sticks.

Lowlight: Newport County AFC 2-1 Leeds United
After exiting the FA Cup at non-league Sutton United in 2017, Leeds were hoping the same fate would not be suffered against Newport County AFC. Having beaten Newport 5-1 in the Carabao Cup earlier in the season, Leeds made a great start when Gaetano Berardi scored his first goal for the club with a long range effort. However a Conor Shaughnessy own goal saw the tie drawn level and Shawn McCoulsky's late winner sent Leeds crashing out.

FEBRUARY

Saturday 3rd February
Sky Bet Championship
Leeds United 1
(Bamba OG 54)
Cardiff City 4
(Paterson 9, Hoilett 41, Morrison 45+5, Pilkington 88)
Venue: Elland Road
Attendance: 30,534

Saturday 10th February
Sky Bet Championship
Sheffield United 2
(Sharp 2, pen 73)
Leeds United 1
(Lasogga 47)
Venue: Bramall Lane
Attendance: 27,553

Sunday 18th February
Sky Bet Championship
Leeds United 2
(Lasogga 72, Roofe 80)
Bristol City 2
(Diedhiou 11, Reid 16)
Venue: Elland Road
Attendance: 28,004

Wednesday 21st February
Sky Bet Championship
Derby County 2
(Weimann 45+2, Palmer 90+2)
Leeds United 2
(Lasogga 34, Alioski 79)
Venue: Pride Park
Attendance: 27,934

Saturday 24th February
Sky Bet Championship
Leeds United 1
(Cooper 31)
Brentford 0
Venue: Elland Road
Attendance: 28,428

Highlight: Leeds United 1-0 Brentford
Paul Heckingbottom left Barnsley to become Leeds United head coach, taking over the reins from Thomas Christiansen and he secured his first win over Brentford at Elland Road. Captain Liam Cooper scored the only goal of the game, heading home a fine free-kick from Ezgjan Alioski. Pierre-Michel Lasogga almost added a second when he went through on goal, but saw his effort cleared off the line, as the single goal proved to be enough.

Lowlight: Leeds United 1-4 Cardiff City
Leeds United suffered a heavy defeat at home against Championship high flyers Cardiff City, which proved to be Thomas Christiansen's last game in charge of the club. The Bluebirds scored two early goals, before Gaetano Berardi was sent off. Sean Morrison added a third before the break and Anthony Pilkington sealed the win late on. An own goal from former Leeds defender Sol Bamba was the only consolation for Leeds on a miserable afternoon.

MARCH

Friday 2nd March
Sky Bet Championship
Middlesbrough 3
(Bamford 31, 36, 68)
Leeds United 0
Venue: Riverside Stadium
Attendance: 27,621

Wednesday 7th March
Sky Bet Championship
Leeds United 0
Wolverhampton Wanderers 3
(Saiss 28, Boly 45, Afobe 74)
Venue: Elland Road
Attendance: 26,434

Saturday 10th March
Sky Bet Championship
Reading 2
(Bodvarsson 16, Kane OG 58)
Leeds United 2
(Jansson 43, Hernández 56)
Venue: Madejski Stadium
Attendance: 19,770

Saturday 17th March
Sky Bet Championship
Leeds United 1
(Grot 86)
Sheffield Wednesday 2
(Nuhiu 71, 90+1)
Venue: Elland Road
Attendance: 31,639

Friday 30th March
Sky Bet Championship
Leeds United 2
*(Ekuban 4,
Hernández 50)*
Bolton Wanderers 1
(Le Fondre 53)
Venue: Elland Road
Attendance: 35,377

Highlight: Leeds United 2-1 Bolton Wanderers
After going four games without a win, Leeds got back to winning ways with a 2-1 victory over Bolton Wanderers. Striker Caleb Ekuban converted a Pierre-Michel Lasogga low cross to give the Whites an early lead. In the second half, Leeds went further ahead, when Pablo Hernández netted, slotting home the rebound from a long range Ezgjan Alioski effort. Adam Le Fondre pulled a goal back for the Trotters, but Leeds held on for the win.

Lowlight: Middlesbrough 3-0 Leeds United
Following a big downpour of snow across the country, an extensive clean up operation was required at the Riverside Stadium and surrounding areas for the game to go ahead. Middlesbrough managed to get the game on, in what was a freezing Friday night in the North East. It proved to be a bad trip all around for the Whites, who suffered a 3-0 defeat, with Boro striker Patrick Bamford netting a hat-trick.

APRIL

Tuesday 3rd April
Sky Bet Championship
Fulham 2
(McDonald 33, Mitrovic 63)
Leeds United 0
Venue: Craven Cottage
Attendance: 21,538

Saturday 7th April
Sky Bet Championship
Leeds United 1
(Hernández 72)
Sunderland 1
(McNair 48)
Venue: Elland Road
Attendance: 30,416

Tuesday 10th April
Sky Bet Championship
Preston North End 3
(Gallagher pen 49, Maguire 52, Browne 82)
Leeds United 1
(Roofe 13)
Venue: Deepdale
Attendance: 14,188

Friday 13th April
Sky Bet Championship
Aston Villa 1
(Grabban 29)
Leeds United 0
Venue: Villa Park
Attendance: 33,374

Saturday 21st April
Sky Bet Championship
Leeds United 2
(Pearce 17, Alioski 50)
Barnsley 1
(O'Connor OG 36)
Venue: Elland Road
Attendance: 30,451

Saturday 28th April
Sky Bet Championship
Norwich City 2
(Hoolahan 45, Murphy 69)
Leeds United 1
(Phillips 49)
Venue: Carrow Road
Attendance: 26,869

Highlight: Leeds United 2-1 Barnsley
Paul Heckingbottom guided Leeds to victory against his former club Barnsley at Elland Road. Tom Pearce opened the scoring in the 17th minute, when he drove up the pitch before finding the bottom corner from range, his first goal for the club. A Paudie O'Connor own goal ensured the two sides went into the break level, but Leeds sealed the win when Kemar Roofe got to the byline and teed up Ezgjan Alioski who fired home.

Lowlight: Preston North End 3-1 Leeds United
Leeds travelled to Deepdale to take on Preston North End in midweek and made a bright start, going ahead through Kemar Roofe, who slotted home following a Kalvin Phillips low drive into the box. However three second half goals saw Preston come back to win the match. Billy Bodin won the home side a penalty, which Paul Gallagher converted early into the second period, before headers from Sean Maguire and Alan Browne sealed the victory.

MAY

Sunday 6th May
Sky Bet Championship
Leeds United 2
(Roofe 30, Phillips 47)
Queens Park Rangers 0
Venue: Elland Road
Attendance: 30,004

The Whites ended the campaign with a 2-0 victory over Queens Park Rangers at Elland Road, thanks to goals in either half from Kemar Roofe and Kalvin Phillips. The result saw Leeds finish in 13th place in the Sky Bet Championship.

	Team	Played	Won	Drawn	Lost	For	Against	GD	Points
1	**Wolverhampton Wanderers**	46	30	9	7	82	39	43	99
2	**Cardiff City**	46	27	9	10	69	39	30	90
3	**Fulham**	46	25	13	8	79	46	33	88
4	**Aston Villa**	46	24	11	11	72	42	30	83
5	**Middlesbrough**	46	22	10	14	67	45	22	76
6	**Derby County**	46	20	15	11	70	48	22	75
7	**Preston North End**	46	19	16	11	57	46	11	73
8	**Millwall**	46	19	15	12	56	45	11	72
9	**Brentford**	46	18	15	13	62	52	10	69
10	**Sheffield United**	46	20	9	17	62	55	7	69
11	**Bristol City**	46	17	16	13	67	58	9	67
12	**Ipswich Town**	46	17	9	20	57	60	-3	60
13	**Leeds United**	46	17	9	20	59	64	-5	60
14	**Norwich City**	46	15	15	16	49	60	-11	60
15	**Sheffield Wednesday**	46	14	15	17	59	60	-1	57
16	**Queens Park Rangers**	46	15	11	20	58	70	-12	56
17	**Nottingham Forest**	46	15	8	23	51	65	-14	53
18	**Hull City**	46	11	16	19	70	70	0	49
19	**Birmingham City**	46	13	7	26	38	68	-30	46
20	**Reading**	46	10	14	22	48	70	-22	44
21	**Bolton Wanderers**	46	10	13	23	39	74	-35	43
22	**Barnsley**	46	9	14	23	48	72	-24	41
23	**Burton Albion**	46	10	11	25	38	81	-43	41
24	**Sunderland**	46	7	16	23	52	80	-28	37

JUNE

Following a post season tour of Myanmar, in June, Leeds United parted company with head coach Paul Heckingbottom, ensuring the 2018/19 campaign would begin with a new man at the helm.

PHENOMENAL SUPPORT

The support Leeds United receive both at home and away is incredible. Here we take a look at the fans in action during the 2017/18 season - thank you, as always, for your fantastic support!

4,832
v Bolton Wanderers (A)
6th August 2017

2,043
v Millwall (A)
16th September 2017

1,993
v Nottingham Forest (A)
26th August 2017

33,771
v Middlesbrough (H)
19th November 2017

3,717
v Bristol City (A)
21st October 2017

3,537
v Ipswich Town
13th January 2018

4,461
v Barnsley (A)
25th November 2017

3,967
v Reading (A)
10th March 2018

35,337
v Bolton Wanderers (H)
30th March 2018

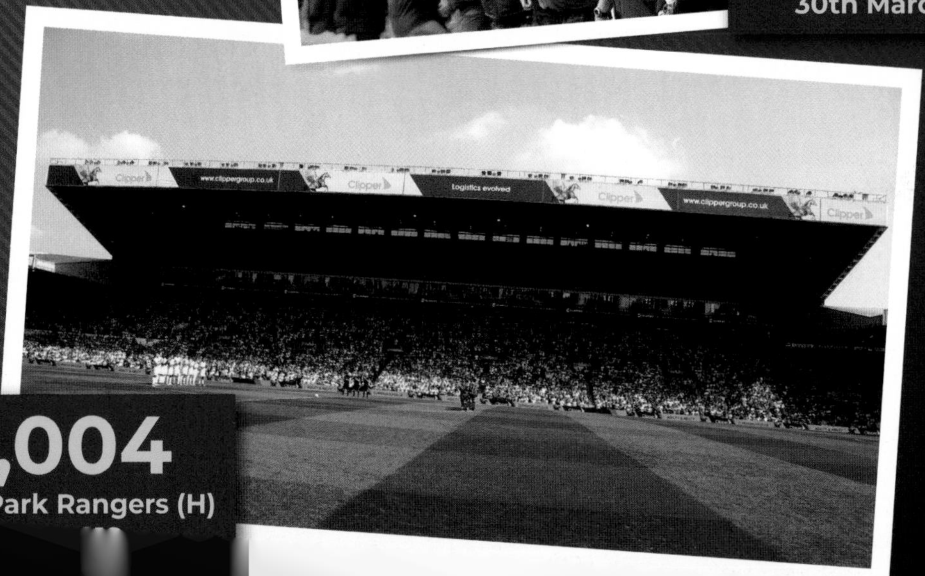

30,004
v Queens Park Rangers (H)

END OF SEASON AWARDS

The Winners

We take a look at whose performances were rewarded with silverware at the end of the 2017/18 season...

PLAYER OF THE YEAR

Pablo Hernández

The midfielder capped off a fine individual season for the Whites, by picking up the Player of the Year Award. The Spaniard was the standout performer of the campaign and was rewarded with a new two year contract before the season came to a close. Hernández missed the awards ceremony, due the birth of his second child.

PLAYERS' PLAYER OF THE YEAR

Pablo Hernández

As well as picking up the Player of the Year Award, Hernández was named the Players' Player of the Year by his team mates. Hernández made a total of 43 appearances for the Whites during the campaign, scoring nine goals.

YOUNG PLAYER OF THE YEAR

Bailey Peacock-Farrell

The goalkeeper was handed just his second start in the defeat against Wolverhampton Wanderers in March, but never looked back with some fine performances between the sticks and went on to earn his first international cap with Northern Ireland in the summer.

GOAL OF THE SEASON

Ezgjan Alioski

v Nottingham Forest

The Macedonian's strike against Nottingham Forest in August was named the Sky Bet Championship goal of the month and also topped a fan poll for Leeds United's Goal of the Season.

LEEDS UNITED LADIES PLAYER OF THE YEAR

Cath Hamill

Captain Cath Hamill was named Leeds United Ladies Player of the Year. Leeds Ladies rejoined forces with Leeds United in the summer of 2017, with exciting plans for the future.

SPECIAL ACHIEVEMENT AWARD

The Leeds United Under-18s picked up the Special Achievement Award at the End of Season Awards. Mark Jackson's Academy side won the Under-18s Professional Development North league title - a fantastic achievement.

BOBBY COLLINS AWARD

Stix Lockwood

An award for outstanding contribution to Leeds United behind the scenes, popular staff member Stix Lockwood picked up this year's Bobby Collins Award.

LIFETIME ACHIEVEMENT AWARD

Peter Lorimer

A new award introduced at this year's ceremony, record goal scorer Peter Lorimer picked up the Lifetime Achievement Award. Peter made his debut at just 15 and, as a player, was part of the club's most successful period in history, remaining as an ambassador of Leeds United today.

BILLY BREMNER XI

Over the summer, a redevelopment of the Billy Bremner Statue has taken place. As part of the redevelopment, fans were asked to vote for 10 players, who would make up the Billy Bremner XI. At the ceremony, the 10 players who topped the fan vote were inducted into the Billy Bremner XI. They were:

Billy Bremner

John Charles	**Jack Charlton**	**Allan Clarke**	**Johnny Giles**	**Eddie Gray**
Norman Hunter	**Peter Lorimer**	**Lucas Radebe**	**Gary Speed**	**Gordon Strachan**

PAST PLAYER OF THE YEAR WINNERS

1971 Norman Hunter	1983 Kenny Burns	1995 Brian Deane	2007 Eddie Lewis
1972 Peter Lorimer	1984 Tommy Wright	1996 Tony Yeboah	2008 Jermaine Beckford
1973 Allan Clarke	1985 Neil Aspin	1997 Nigel Martyn	2009 Jermaine Beckford
1974 Mick Jones	1986 Ian Snodin	1998 Lucas Radebe	2010 Patrick Kisnorbo
1975 Gordon McQueen	1987 John Sheridan	1999 Lee Bowyer	2011 Max Gradel
1976 Paul Madeley	1988 Peter Haddock	2000 Harry Kewell	2012 Robert Snodgrass
1977 Gordon McQueen	1989 Ian Baird	2001 Lee Bowyer	2013 Sam Byram
1978 Tony Currie	1990 Chris Fairclough	2002 Rio Ferdinand	2014 Ross McCormack
1979 Brian Flynn	1991 David Batty	2003 Paul Robinson	2015 Alex Mowatt
1980 John Lukic	1992 Tony Dorigo	2004 Alan Smith	2016 Charlie Taylor
1981 Trevor Cherry	1993 Gordon Strachan	2005 Neil Sullivan	2017 Chris Wood
1982 Eddie Gray	1994 Gary McAllister	2006 Gary Kelly	

A LOOK BACK AT THE CLOS

There have once again been many changes at Elland Road and Thorp Arch over the close season.

The biggest change saw Marcelo Bielsa named head coach of the club, with the former Argentina and Chile boss replacing Paul Heckingbottom at the helm, sparking attention across the globe.

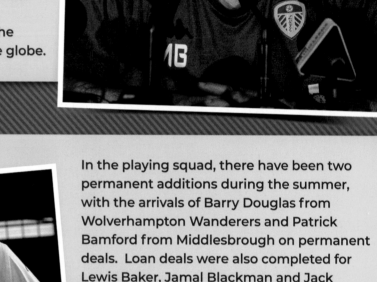

In the playing squad, there have been two permanent additions during the summer, with the arrivals of Barry Douglas from Wolverhampton Wanderers and Patrick Bamford from Middlesbrough on permanent deals. Loan deals were also completed for Lewis Baker, Jamal Blackman and Jack Harrison ahead of the 2018/19 campaign, from Premier League sides Chelsea and Manchester City respectively.

The squad has also been trimmed by a number of departures, with Marcus Antonsson, Madger Gomes, Andy Lonergan, Luke Murphy, Ronaldo Vieira and Felix Wiedwald leaving permanently. A number of players have also departed on loan including Lewie Coyle, Pawel Cibicki, Laurens De Bock, Caleb Ekuban, Jay-Roy Grot, Yosuke Ideguchi, Paudie O'Connor and Hadi Sacko.

SEASON

Away from the pitch, at Elland Road, the first phase of the Bremner Square project has been completed, with the area around the statue of the club's most famous player completely refurbished. Bremner Square was officially opened in July by club legends Eddie Gray, Norman Hunter and Peter Lorimer. Over 6,000 personalised stones created by Leeds United supporters have been installed and will now remain part of the club's history. Further installations are expected to be carried out once again throughout 2019!

A number of changes have also been made to the hospitality suites at Elland Road, with two brand new areas opened ahead of the 2018/19 campaign.

New club shops have also opened across the city recently, with new stores at Trinity Leeds and Leeds Bradford International Airport, giving more Leeds United supporters the opportunity to get hold of merchandise. The superstore at Elland Road has also been completely refurbished, so if you haven't already, make sure you check it out!

An investment by USA NFL side San Francisco 49ers was also made in the club over the close season, with Paraag Marathe joining Andrea Radrizzani, Ivan Bravo, Angus Kinnear and Andre Tegner on the Board of Directors.

ALL LEEDS.

2018/19 HOME KIT
ON SALE NOW

2018/19 KIT LAUNCH

Our 2018/19 home kit was unveiled at a number of exclusive events for Season Ticket Holders at our club shops at Elland Road, Leeds Trinity, Leeds Bradford Airport and the Merrion Centre.

A selection of players were on hand at each location, along with chairman Andrea Radrizzani, to celebrate the launch of the kit and met a large number of supporters in the process. Our club photographer captured the action.

MARCELO BIELSA

A background on Leeds United's head coach

Marcelo Bielsa is a household name amongst football fans across the world, due to his tactics, style of play and approach, so his appointment at Leeds United sparked interest across the globe.

Bielsa's management career began following his retirement from playing; his first professional management job was with Newell's Old Boys in his homeland of Argentina. Whilst at Newell's Old Boys he won the Argentinean Primera División Apertura in 1991 and Clausura in 1992. His success led to the club naming their stadium after him in 2009.

In 1992, Bielsa left Newell's and managed Atlas and Club América in Mexico, before returning to his homeland to take over Vélez Sársfield, where he guided them to first place in the Clausura in 1998.

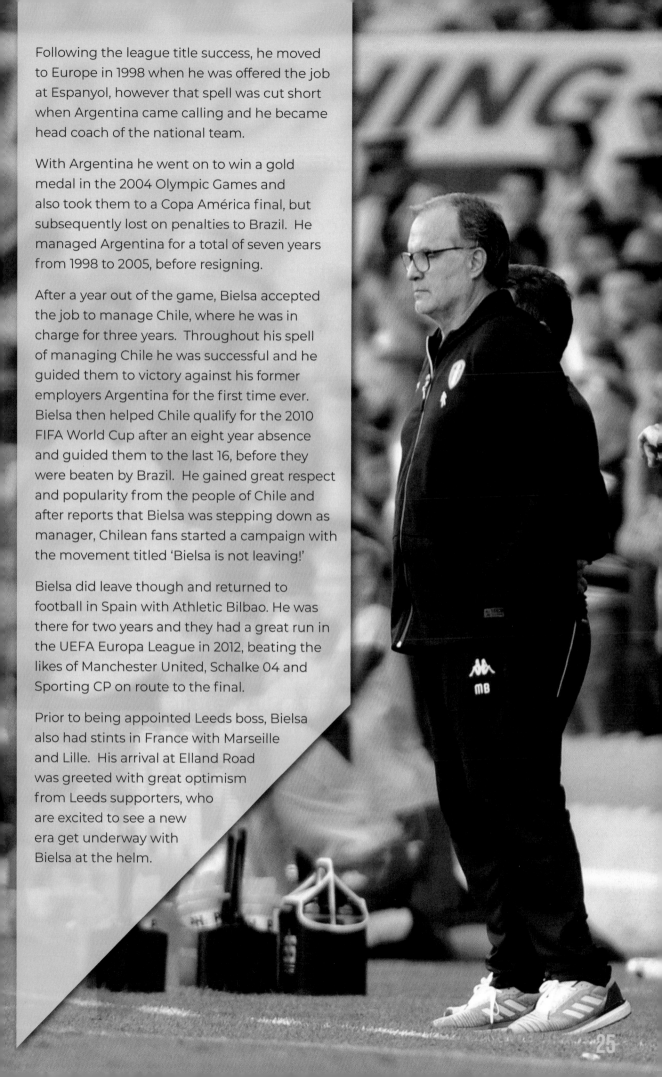

Following the league title success, he moved to Europe in 1998 when he was offered the job at Espanyol, however that spell was cut short when Argentina came calling and he became head coach of the national team.

With Argentina he went on to win a gold medal in the 2004 Olympic Games and also took them to a Copa América final, but subsequently lost on penalties to Brazil. He managed Argentina for a total of seven years from 1998 to 2005, before resigning.

After a year out of the game, Bielsa accepted the job to manage Chile, where he was in charge for three years. Throughout his spell of managing Chile he was successful and he guided them to victory against his former employers Argentina for the first time ever. Bielsa then helped Chile qualify for the 2010 FIFA World Cup after an eight year absence and guided them to the last 16, before they were beaten by Brazil. He gained great respect and popularity from the people of Chile and after reports that Bielsa was stepping down as manager, Chilean fans started a campaign with the movement titled 'Bielsa is not leaving!'

Bielsa did leave though and returned to football in Spain with Athletic Bilbao. He was there for two years and they had a great run in the UEFA Europa League in 2012, beating the likes of Manchester United, Schalke 04 and Sporting CP on route to the final.

Prior to being appointed Leeds boss, Bielsa also had stints in France with Marseille and Lille. His arrival at Elland Road was greeted with great optimism from Leeds supporters, who are excited to see a new era get underway with Bielsa at the helm.

PLAYER PROFILES

GOALKEEPERS

BAILEY PEACOCK-FARRELL

Squad Number: 1
Nationality: Northern Irish
Date of Birth: 29/10/1996

Goalkeeper Bailey Peacock-Farrell joined Leeds from Middlesbrough's Academy back in 2013 and went on to make his first team debut against Queens Park Rangers in April 2016.

After being a regular in the matchday squad throughout the rest of 2016 and 2017, Peacock-Farrell went on to make a second Whites appearance against Wolverhampton Wanderers in March 2018.

His performance against Wolves saw Peacock-Farrell retain his place between the sticks for the Whites for rest of the 2017/18 season and at the end of the campaign, he earned a first senior cap for Northern Ireland.

JAMAL BLACKMAN

Squad Number: 27
Nationality: English
Date of Birth: 27/10/1993

Jamal Blackman became Leeds United's second signing of the 2018 summer transfer window when he joined from Chelsea on a season-long loan.

The 24-year-old goalkeeper knows the Sky Bet Championship well, having spent the 2017/18 season at fellow Yorkshire side Sheffield United, where he made 33 appearances and kept nine clean sheets.

Blackman has been capped at various youth levels by England and has also had temporary stints away from Stamford Bridge at Östersunds and Wycombe Wanderers.

LUKE AYLING

Squad Number: 2
Nationality: English
Date of Birth: 25/08/1991

Popular full-back Luke Ayling joined the Whites from Sky Bet Championship rivals Bristol City in the summer of 2016.

Ayling began his career at Arsenal and progressed through the ranks, before moving to Yeovil Town in 2010, helping the Glovers achieve promotion from League One in 2013.

He was snapped up by Bristol City the following year and also helped the Robins secure a return to the Championship from League One.

Ayling signed a new four year deal with the club in October 2017, committing his future to the Whites until 2021.

GAETANO BERARDI

Squad Number: 28
Nationality: Swiss
Date of Birth: 21/08/1988

The Swiss full-back signed for Leeds from Italian outfit Sampdoria in July 2014.

Berardi, who is equally as comfortable playing on the right or the left, endured a testing start to life in English football and was sent off on his United debut, but the defender's solid performances have established him as a key figure in the side.

Berardi twice won the Play-Offs during his time in Serie B – with Brescia and Sampdoria.

He has earned a cult hero status at Elland Road for his commitment to the cause.

PLAYER PROFILES

DEFENDERS

LIAM COOPER

Squad Number: 6
Nationality: Scottish
Date of Birth: 30/08/1991

The centre-back joined the club from Chesterfield in summer 2014 after catching the eye in a pre-season friendly against the Whites.

Cooper, a product of Hull City's Academy, has been a regular fixture at the heart of the United defence since his arrival and his performances have led to call-ups to the senior Scotland squad.

The left-sided centre-back previously spent time on loan at Carlisle United and Huddersfield Town while on the books of Hull, before earning a place in the League Two PFA Team of the Year 2013/14 as he helped Chesterfield secure promotion.

BARRY DOUGLAS

Squad Number: 3
Nationality: Scottish
Date of Birth: 04/09/1989

Barry Douglas signed for Leeds United from Wolverhampton Wanderers in July 2018 for an undisclosed fee.

Starting his career at Queens Park, Douglas also had stints with Dundee United, Lech Poznan and Konyaspor.

He joined Leeds having helped Wolves to win promotion from the Sky Bet Championship in the previous season.

No player provided more assists than Douglas in the Championship during the 2017/18 campaign and he will be hoping to continue that form at Elland Road.

PONTUS JANSSON

Squad Number: 18
Nationality: Swedish
Date of Birth: 13/02/1991

Swedish international defender Pontus Jansson arrived at Leeds initially on a season-long loan from Italian outfit Torino, before the move was made permanent in 2017.

The six-foot-five centre-back began his career with homeland outfit Malmö FF, before moving to Torino in 2014.

Jansson regularly features on the international stage for Sweden and played at the 2018 FIFA World Cup in Russia.

TOM PEARCE

Squad Number: 20
Nationality: English
Date of Birth: 12/04/1998

Tom Pearce started his youth career at Everton, before joining Leeds United.

Since joining Leeds, Pearce has been a regular for United's Academy and his impressive performances led to a senior debut against Sheffield Wednesday in March 2018.

He committed his long term future to Leeds United by signing a new four year contract at the end of the 2017/18 season.

MIDFIELDERS

EZGJAN ALIOSKI

Squad Number: 10
Nationality: Macedonian
Date of Birth: 12/02/1992

Leeds United moved to sign Ezgjan Alioski from Swiss side Lugano for an undisclosed fee in the summer of 2017.

The attacking midfielder has also had spells at fellow Swiss sides Young Boys and Schaffhausen. On the international stage, Alioski is a regular starter for Macedonia and has over 15 caps to his name.

In his first season at the Whites, Alioski made 45 appearances in all competitions, more than any other player, and scored seven goals.

PLAYER PROFILES

MIDFIELDERS

LEWIS BAKER

Squad Number: 34
Nationality: English
Date of Birth: 25/04/1995

Leeds United completed the signing of Lewis Baker from Premier League side Chelsea on a season-long loan in June 2018.

A product of Chelsea's Academy, the midfielder has had a number of loan spells away from Stamford Bridge previously, with stints at MK Dons, Vitesse Arnhem and Middlesbrough.

At Vitesse, Baker helped the Eredivisie side win the Dutch Cup for the first time in 2017 and has also been capped at various youth levels by England, including 17 times for the Under-21s where he scored eight goals.

STUART DALLAS

Squad Number: 15
Nationality: Northern Irish
Date of Birth: 19/04/1991

The Northern Ireland international soon settled into life at Elland Road following his summer 2015 move from Brentford, ending his debut campaign as United's Players' Player of the Year.

Dallas, who began his career with semi-professional homeland side Crusaders, became the first United player to feature in a major tournament for 10 years when he represented his country at Euro 2016.

The winger, a League One promotion winner with Brentford in 2014, signed a new three year contract with the Whites in August 2017.

ADAM FORSHAW

Squad Number: 4
Nationality: English
Date of Birth: 08/10/1991

Midfielder Adam Forshaw joined Leeds United in January 2018 from fellow Championship side Middlesbrough, signing a four and a half year deal with the Whites.

Forshaw came through ranks at Everton, before moving to Brentford, where he was named League One Player of the Year in 2014, after helping the Bees win promotion.

A short spell at Wigan Athletic followed, before he joined Middlesbrough in January 2015, helping them win promotion to the Premier League the following season.

JACK HARRISON

Squad Number: 22
Nationality: English
Date of Birth: 20/11/1996

Jack Harrison joined Leeds United on a season-long loan ahead of the 2018/19 campaign from Premier League champions Manchester City.

The winger had spells at Liverpool and Manchester United as a youngster, before joining New York City.

During his time in Major League Soccer, Harrison made 57 appearances and scored 14 goals for the Yankee Stadium outfit, resulting in a move to partner club Manchester City in January 2018.

PLAYER PROFILES

MIDFIELDERS

PABLO HERNANDEZ

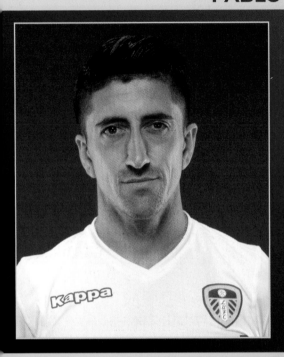

Squad Number: 19
Nationality: Spanish
Date of Birth: 11/04/1985

Spanish attacking midfielder Pablo Hernandez joined the Whites initially on loan from Qatari side Al-Arabi in 2016, before signing a permanent deal.

The vastly-experienced Hernandez came through the ranks at Valencia and arrived at Elland Road with over 130 La Liga appearances to his name and four full international caps.

Hernandez, who also had spells at Getafe, Swansea City and Rayo Vallecano, picked up the Leeds United Player of the Year Award and signed a new two year contract at the end of the 2017/18 campaign.

MATEUSZ KLICH

Squad Number: 43
Nationality: Polish
Date of Birth: 13/06/1990

Polish international midfielder Mateusz Klich joined Leeds United from Dutch outfit FC Twente in the summer of 2017.

Starting his career at Polish outfit KS Cracovia, Klich has had spells in Germany with VfL Wolfsburg and 1. FC Kaiserslautern and in the Netherlands with PEC Zwolle and FC Twente.

Klich spent the second half of the 2017/18 campaign on loan with Eredivisie side FC Utrecht.

KALVIN PHILLIPS

Squad Number: 23
Nationality: English
Date of Birth: 02/12/1995

The home grown midfielder scored on his Elland Road debut in April 2015 against Cardiff City - just five days after making his first senior appearance away at Wolverhampton Wanderers.

Phillips, who joined the club from local side Wortley Juniors in 2010, progressed through the ranks at Thorp Arch and earned a glowing reputation for his all-action displays prior to his first-team breakthrough.

During the 2017/18 season, Phillips chipped in with seven goals, but is expected to play a deeper role under new head coach Marcelo Bielsa.

SAMUEL SÁIZ

Squad Number: 14
Nationality: Spanish
Date of Birth: 22/01/1991

Exciting midfielder Samuel Sáiz signed for Leeds United from Spanish outfit Huesca on a four year contract in the summer of 2017 for an undisclosed fee.

Born in Madrid, Sáiz came through the ranks at Spanish giants Real, going on to make appearances for their B and C teams.

Spells at UD Melilla, Getafe, UD Almería and Atlético Madrid followed, before he joined Huesca.

JAMIE SHACKLETON

Squad Number: 46
Nationality: English
Date of Birth: 08/10/1999

Jamie Shackleton is the latest player to progress through the Leeds United Academy to the first team.

After featuring regularly for the Under-18s and Under-23s, Shackleton impressed for the Whites during pre-season ahead of the 2018/19 campaign.

He made his debut for Leeds against Derby County in August 2018 and made his first start against Bolton Wanderers at Elland Road three days later.

PLAYER PROFILES

PATRICK BAMFORD

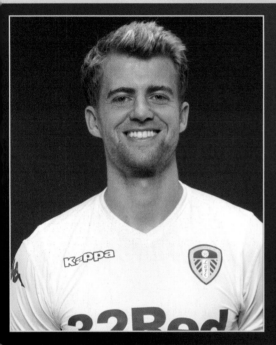

Squad Number: 9
Nationality: English
Date of Birth: 05/09/1993

Leeds United completed the signing of striker Patrick Bamford from Sky Bet Championship rivals Middlesbrough for an undisclosed fee on 31st July 2018, signing a four year deal with the Whites.

An England youth international, Bamford started his career with Nottingham Forest before being snapped up by Chelsea.

He had a number of loan spells away from Stamford Bridge and at Middlesbrough was named the 2014/15 Sky Bet Championship Player of the Year.

Further temporary spells at Crystal Palace, Norwich City and Burnley followed, before a move back to the Riverside permanently and he scored a hat-trick against Leeds for Boro in March 2018.

RYAN EDMONDSON

Squad Number: 39
Nationality: English
Date of Birth: 20/05/2001

Promising striker Ryan Edmondson signed for Leeds United in November 2017 for an undisclosed fee from National League North side York City as a 16-year-old.

Edmondson, who made senior appearances with the Minstermen, was named captain of the Under-18s and helped them win the Professional Development League North in his first season.

His performances saw him make a senior debut on the last day of the 2017/18 season against Queens Park Rangers.

TYLER ROBERTS

Squad Number: 11
Nationality: Welsh
Date of Birth: 12/01/1999

Leeds United signed Tyler Roberts in January 2018 from then Premier League side West Bromwich Albion.

The forward, who has been capped by Wales at youth level put pen to paper on a four and a half year deal at Elland Road, running until the summer of 2022.

Roberts made his debut for the Baggies in the 1-1 Premier League draw with Liverpool back in May 2016 and has also had temporary stints at Oxford United and Shrewsbury Town and Walsall, gaining valuable first team experience.

KEMAR ROOFE

Squad Number: 7
Nationality: English
Date of Birth: 06/01/1993

Kemar Roofe signed a four year deal upon joining the Whites from Oxford United in the summer of 2016.

Roofe, a former West Bromwich Albion trainee, established himself as one of the Football League's hottest properties during 2015/16 as he helped fire his side to promotion to League One with 26 goals from 49 appearances and his performances earned him the League Two Player of the Year Award .

The versatile attacker has previously spent time on loan at Icelandic side Vikingur Reykjavik, as well as homeland clubs Northampton Town, Cheltenham Town and Colchester United.

PRE-SEASON

PREPARATIONS FOR THE 2018/19 SEASON

Leeds United played six pre-season friendlies ahead of the 2018/19 Sky Bet Championship campaign, with five games on the road and one match at Elland Road. Here is how the Whites got on...

TUESDAY 17TH JULY 2018

Forest Green Rovers 1 (Grubb 45+1)
Leeds United 2 (Roofe 16, Ayling 25)

Forest Green: Montgomery, Shephard, James (Trialist 74), Rawson (Hollis 68), Winchester (Simpson 76), Grubb, Doidge, Williams (Arcibald), Gunning, Mills (Laird 68), Reid (Brown 45). Subs not used: Thomas.

Leeds: Peacock-Farrell, Ayling, Cooper, Berardi, Forshaw, Phillips, Dallas, Alioski, Saiz, Hernandez, Roofe. Subs not used: Miazek, Dalby, Diaz, Rey.

Venue: New Lawn
Attendance: 3,250
Referee: S. Allison
Star man: Luke Ayling

After missing a large part of last season with injury, Ayling was back to his very best against Forest Green Rovers in the first game of pre-season. He was a constant threat up and down the right wing and netted a rare goal.

THURSDAY 19TH JULY 2018

York City 1 (Trialist 23)
Leeds United 1 (Dalby 57)

York: Bartlett, Griffiths (Law 61), Newton, Bencherif, Trialist (Parslow 45), Penn (Moke 61), York (Steels 66), Heslop, Burrow (Wright 61), Kempster (Ferguson 61), Longstaff (Parkin 61). Subs not used: Whitley.

Leeds: Miazek (Huffer 45), De Bock, Ideguchi, Vieira, Baker, Klich, Pearce, Clarke, Edmondson (Dalby 45), Shackleton, Stevens (Diaz 45). Subs not used: Rey.

Venue: Bootham Crescent
Attendance: 4,400
Referee: R. Joyce
Star man: Jamie Shackleton

Marcelo Bielsa named a youthful side for the trip to York City and 18-year-old Jamie Shackleton was a constant threat going forward. He was unlucky not to score in the second half, but was denied by a fine save from Adam Bartlett.

SUNDAY 22ND JULY 2018

Southend United 1 (Lennon 20)

Leeds United 1 (Ayling 34)

Southend: Oxley, Demetriou, Coker (Hendrie 84), Lennon (Turner 76), White (Kyprianou 84), Mantom, (Batlokwa 69), Dieng (Hyam 9) (Klass 76), Kightly (Barratt 69), McLaughlin (Bwomono 84), Cox (Ba 69), Hopper (Robinson 69). Subs not used: Bishop.

Leeds: Peacock-Farrell, Ayling, Cooper, De Bock (Roberts 62), Berardi, Forshaw, Phillips, Alioski, Saiz, Dallas, Roofe. Subs not used: Miazek, Edmondson, Stevens.

Venue: Roots Hall

Attendance: 3,815 (988 Leeds)

Referee: G. Ward

Star man: Adam Forshaw

The midfielder played a fine one-two with Luke Ayling in the build up to Leeds' goal, which split the Southend defence. He was a calming presence in the centre of the park at Roots Hall and his slick passing led to decent opportunities for the Whites.

TUESDAY 24TH JULY 2018

Oxford United 4 (Henry 7, 43 Hall 26, Obika 61)

Leeds United 3 (Roberts 54, Baker 63, Clarke 71)

Oxford: Eastwood, Norman, Dickie (Raglan 81), Mousinho, Garbutt, Ruffels (Carroll 81), Brannagan (Nelson 74), Hall (Napa 46), Henry (Mackie 70), Carruthers (Baptiste 74), Obika (Lopes 83). Subs not used: Shearer, Long.

Leeds: Huffer (Blackman 45), Shackleton, Diaz, Rey, Pearce, Klich, Vieira, Ideguchi (Roberts 45), Baker, Clarke, Dalby (Edmondson 45). Subs not used: Stevens.

Venue: Kassam Stadium

Attendance: 4,727 (1,336 Leeds)

Referee: A. Coggins

Star man: Tyler Roberts

Introduced at half time at the Kassam Stadium, Roberts had an almost instant impact, netting his first Leeds goal with a fine curling effort. The Whites looked a lot more of a threat with him on the pitch as he stepped up his comeback from injury.

THURSDAY 26TH JULY 2018

Guiseley 3 (Clayton 3, Thompson 29, Trialist A 73)

Leeds United 4 (Klich 39, Clarke 49, Edmondson 53, 71)

Guiseley: Green, Moyo (Hatfield 38), Purver, Heaton (Trialist B 77) Thornton, Kennedy (Morrison 45), James, Liburd (Trialist A 61), Clayton (Odejayi 73), Thompson (Smith 61), Halls. Subsnot used: Worsnop, Smith, Harvery, Flowers, Trialist C, Trialist D, Paley.

Leeds: Blackman, Shackleton, De Bock, Diaz (Rey 68), Pearce, Klich, Vieira, Clarke, Baker, Roberts (Stevens 38), Edmondson (Dalby 72). Subs not used: Miazek, Ideguchi.

Venue: Nethermoor Park

Attendance: 3,366

Referee: J. Moss

Star man: Ryan Edmondson

The 17-year-old striker netted two second half goals against Guiseley to secure Leeds victory at Nethermoor Park. His first was a calm and composed first time finish to put Leeds 3-2 ahead, before he netted with a bullet header in the 71st minute to wrap up the comeback win.

SUNDAY 29TH JULY 2018

Leeds United 1 (Roofe 86)

UD Las Palmas 0

Leeds: Peacock-Farrell, Ayling, Berardi, Cooper, Dallas, Phillips, Vieira (Baker 45) (Shackleton 88), Alioski, Saiz (Klich 45), Hernandez, Roofe. Subs not used: Blackman, Huffer, Roberts, Pearce, Clarke.

Las Palmas: Fernandez, Garcia, Castro (Parras 68), Mir (Benito 59), Araujo (Espiau 78), Lemos (Gomez 81), Fidel (Tana 68), J. Castellano, Cala (Deivid 82, D. Castellano, Fabio. Subs not used: Perez, Momo, Deivid, Suarez, Josep, Curbelo, Exposito, Josemi.

Venue: Elland Road

Attendance: 11,499

Referee: A. Madely

Star man: Kemar Roofe

The striker was on hand to score Leeds United a late winner against UD Las Palmas, to ensure the Whites ended their pre-season campaign with victory. The ball fell to Roofe in the box and he showed fine footwork, before firing home from close range.

THE BIG LEEDS

1 Who was Leeds United's top goal scorer in the 2017/18 campaign?

2 Which team did Adam Forshaw join Leeds United from?

3 Who won Leeds United's Player of the Year Award in 2018?

4 What squad number does Kalvin Phillips wear for Leeds?

5 Which team did forward Tyler Roberts join Leeds United from?

6 What position does Bailey Peacock-Farrell play for Leeds?

7 Jamal Blackman is on loan at Leeds United from which club?

8 What number did club legend Billy Bremner used to wear for Leeds?

9 Which former manager has a statue and stand named after him at Elland Road?

10 What squad number does Stuart Dallas wear for Leeds?

UNITED QUIZ

11 Who was Leeds United's first pre-season game ahead of the 2018/19 season against?

12 What nationality is Samuel Sáiz?

13 Who made the most appearances for Leeds in the 2017/18 season?

14 Who was Leeds United's biggest victory of the 2017/18 season against?

15 What squad number does Pablo Hernandez wear for Leeds?

16 How many times have Leeds United won the League Cup?

17 Leeds United are one of how many teams in the Sky Bet Championship?

18 Which team did Luke Ayling join Leeds United from?

19 What nationality is Mateusz Klich?

20 When did Leeds United last win the First Division (now Premier League)?

GAETANO BERARDI

PLAYER FACTS

LIAM COOPER

1 Joined Leeds United from Wolverhampton Wanderers in July 2018

2 Wears shirt number 28 for Leeds United

JACK HARRISON

PONTUS JANSSON

Can you match the facts with the Leeds United player they belong to?

3 Played for Sweden at the 2018 FIFA World Cup

5 Played in the MLS for New York City and is on loan at Leeds United from Manchester City

BARRY DOUGLAS

GAETANO BERARDI

4 Is the captain of Leeds United and wears squad number 6

NO.	PLAYER

Answers on page 60-61

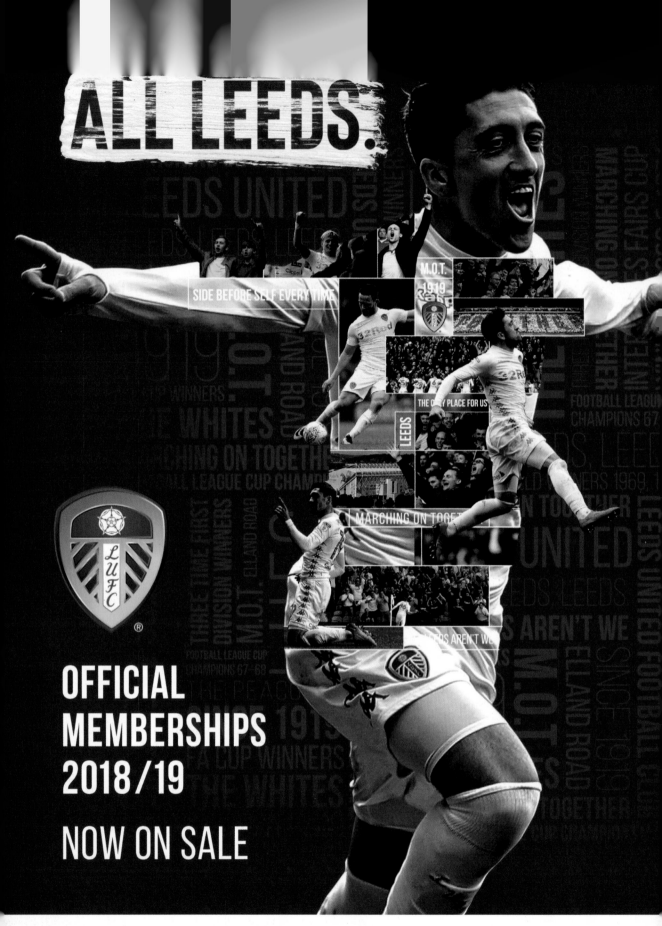

ALL LEEDS.

OFFICIAL MEMBERSHIPS 2018/19

NOW ON SALE

By becoming a Leeds United Member, you'll receive a whole host of exclusive benefits, including exclusive retail offers, priority purchase for home match tickets, and the opportunity to apply for away tickets.

www.leedsunited.com

SPOT THE DIFFERENCE

Can you spot the ten differences in this photo with
Leeds United defender Gaetano Berardi?

DREAM TEAM

Leeds United captain Liam Cooper selects four players to line-up alongside him in a five-a-side dream team. To qualify for selection, Cooper must have played with or against the four players he chooses.

His selections were...

TOMMY LEE

The goalkeeper played with Cooper during his time at Chesterfield, where the duo won promotion from League Two to League One. The shot-stopper made a total of 373 appearances at Chesterfield after joining in 2008, but was forced to retire from the game in November 2017 with a recurring shoulder injury at the age of 31.

STEVEN GERRARD

Now manager of Rangers, Gerrard had a fantastic club career with Liverpool, making his debut in 1998 and remaining a key player until his departure to MLS outfit LA Galaxy in 2015. With the Reds, Gerrard won the FA Cup twice, League Cup three times and both the UEFA Cup and UEFA Champions League.

GEOVANNI

Brazilian attacking midfielder Geovanni had a spell in English football from 2007-2010 with Manchester City and Hull City. He also played for Spanish giants Barcelona and Portugese outfit Benfica. He scored some stunning goals during his time playing in the Premier League and also earned an international cap with Brazil.

JAY-JAY OKACHA

The Nigerian was one of the most skillful players to play in England. He was signed by Bolton Wanderers in 2002 and spent four years with the club, making over 100 appearances. He won 75 caps for Nigeria and joined Hull City in 2007, linking up with Cooper at the Tigers.

EZGJAN ALIOSKI

GOING FOR GOAL

Luke Ayling, Tyler Roberts and Samuel Sáiz are all trying to score, but only one of them can complete the task - can you work out who will find the net?

YOU ARE THE GAFFER:

We spoke to Pablo Hernandez about what he would do if he was in charge for the day. He tells us about the different decisions he would make, which manager he would most be like and who in the current squad would be his right hand man.

Tracksuit or suit?

"Tracksuit."

Formation of choice?

"4-2-3-1"

What style would your team play?

"I would want my team to play with an identity, this would be to play possession-style football and use the wingers to put good crosses into the box."

Which manager would you be most like?

"For me one of the best managers that I have worked with is Michael Laudrup, but I am a big fan of Mauricio Pochettino, I think he is a good manager."

Who in the current Leeds squad would be your assistant manager?

"I could chose three or four, but probably Samuel Sáiz as we can both speak Spanish really well."

PABLO HERNANDEZ

You are playing your main rivals, do you talk them up or play it down?

"I would play it down and keep calm."

What fine would you introduce?

"A fine for using your phone too much."

What team bonding activity would you chose?

"Golf."

You are in the Premier League- would you prefer Champions League qualification or winning the FA Cup?

"Top four and Champions League. I am lucky to have played in the Champions League and it is an unbelievable feeling. It was one of the best moments in my career. I think it is the best club competition in the world."

You can sign any goalkeeper, defender, midfielder and striker in the world, past or present, who are they?

"David de Gea, Sergio Ramos, Isco, Lionel Messi."

SPOT THE BALL

Here's loan signing Lewis Baker in action for Leeds United.
But can you work out where the ball should be?

KALVIN PHILLIPS

CROSSWORD

ACROSS

1. Wears squad number 19 for Leeds United. (5,9)

5. A former player who made 556 appearances for Leeds and can be regularly heard on LUTV. (5,4)

7. The first name of the club's mascot. (5)

12. A former player who captained both Leeds United and South Africa and wore the number 5 shirt. (5,6)

14. The colour of Leeds United's 2018/19 home kit. (5)

15. The colour of Leeds United's 2018/19 away kit. (4)

16. An international team head coach Marcelo Bielsa has managed, other than Chile. (9)

17. Bailey Peacock-Farrell plays international football for this country. (8,7)

DOWN

2. The name of Leeds United Chairman. (6,10)

3. The name of Leeds United's stadium.(6,4)

4. The name of the former player who has a statue in the South East Corner of Elland Road. (5,7)

6. A current team in the Sky Bet Championship other than Leeds United that Pablo Hernandez has played for. (7,4)

8. Patrick Bamford joined Leeds United from this team. (13)

9. Wears squad number two for Leeds United. (4,6)

10. A former manager who left Leeds in 1974 to manage England. (3,5)

11. Ezgjan Alioski plays international football for this country. (9)

13. Leeds United defeated this team on the first day of the 2018/19 Sky Bet Championship season. (5,4)

WORDSEARCH

Can you find the surnames of the 11 Leeds United players who started in our opening game of the 2018/19 season against Stoke City in our wordsearch?

G	M	V	Q	B	M	Z	P	V	M	L	D	P	L
H	C	I	L	K	N	M	T	R	F	L	Z	N	H
V	Y	L	R	O	O	F	E	N	G	E	K	C	K
K	B	E	R	A	R	D	I	N	R	R	R	T	F
F	X	B	T	K	M	T	I	D	D	R	L	I	J
Z	Z	M	T	H	X	L	V	Y	N	A	P	K	K
T	L	E	N	B	Y	Z	B	F	K	F	H	S	W
D	Z	T	D	A	L	R	Q	D	R	K	I	O	V
T	Y	C	B	N	K	R	O	K	Z	C	L	I	Y
F	R	V	O	P	A	U	P	I	X	O	L	L	T
R	K	H	W	O	G	N	A	F	N	C	I	A	K
C	W	F	D	L	P	S	R	C	D	A	P	R	D
Z	L	V	A	F	T	E	R	E	V	E	S	F	R
V	W	S	T	T	M	M	R	C	H	P	D	Q	M

Peacock-Farrell
Ayling
Berardi
Cooper

Phillips
Douglas
Klich

Hernandez
Alioski
Saiz
Roofe

FOR THE RECORD

Club Facts and Figures

Elland Road capacity: 37,890

Elland Road pitch measurements: 115 x 74 yards

Nicknames: 'United' or 'The Whites'

First choice colours: White

2018/19 Change colour: Blue

Leeds United were founded in 1919 but it was 1920 when
the club gained election into the Football League.

First game in Football League: August 28 1920,
Division Two v Port Vale (a) Lost 0-2

Record attendance: 57,892 v Sunderland
FA Cup 5th rnd replay March 15 1967

Record League win: 8-0 v Leicester City, Division One, April 7 1934

Record European win: 10-0 v Lyn Oslo, European Cup
1st rnd 1st leg September 17 1969

Record FA Cup win: 8-1 v Crystal Palace (Rnd 3) January 1930

Record League Cup win: 5-1 v Mansfield Town (Rnd 2), September 1963

Record League defeat: 1-8 v Stoke City, Division One, August 27 1934

Record European defeat: 0-4 v SK Lierse (UEFA Cup) 1st rnd,
1st leg, Sept 1971 / Barcelona (Champs League), Sept 2000

Record FA Cup defeat: 2-7 v Middlesbrough (Rnd 3), January 1946

Record League Cup defeat: 0-7 v West Ham (Rnd 3),
November 1966 / Arsenal (Rnd 2), September 1979

Record League scorer in a season: John Charles 43, Division Two 1953 - 54

Highest number of league goals in a match: 5, Gordon
Hodgson v Leicester City, Division One, October 1 1938

Highest number of League goals in aggregate: Peter Lorimer 168

Record all-time goalscorer: Peter Lorimer 238

Record appearances in league matches: Jack Charlton 629

Record all-time appearances: 773 Jack Charlton / Billy Bremner

Record transfer fee paid: £18m to West Ham
for Rio Ferdinand, November 2000

Record transfer fee received: £29.1m from
Manchester Utd for Rio Ferdinand, July 2002

Oldest Player: Eddie Burbank (41yrs and 23 days)
- v Hull City, April 1954

Youngest Player: Peter Lorimer (15 years and 289 days)
- v Southampton, September 1962

First schoolboy to play for club: Tom Elliott v Norwich City, February 3, 2007

Most players used in a season: 44 (2004/05 and 2006/07)

Match Sequences

Unbeaten start to the season: 29 (1973/74)

Most successive wins in all competitions to start season: 8 (2009/10)

Longest undefeated run: 34 (Oct 1968 - Aug 1969)

Longest undefeated run at home: 39 (May 1968 - March 1970)

Longest undefeated run away: 17 (Oct 1968 - Aug 1969)

Successive home wins (league): 15 (Jan 2009 - Oct 2010)

Successive defeats (league): 6 (April 1947 - May 1947)

Successive games without a win (league): 17 (January 1947 - August 1947)

Longest run without a home win: 10 (February 1982 - May 1982)

Longest run without an away win: 26 (March 1939 - August 1947)

Managers

Dick Ray 1919 - 1920	David O'Leary 1998 - 2002
Arthur Fairclough 1920 - 1927	Terry Venables 2002 - 2003
Dick Ray 1927 - 35	Peter Reid 2003 (Mar - Nov)
Billy Hampson 1935 - 1947	Eddie Gray 2003 - 2004
Willis Edwards 1947 - 1948	Kevin Blackwell 2004 - 2006
Major Frank Buckley 1948 - 1953	Dennis Wise 2006 - 2008
Raich Carter 1953 - 1958	Gary McAllister 2008 (Jan - Dec)
Bill Lambton 1958 - 1959	Simon Grayson 2008 - 2012
Jack Taylor 1959 - 1961	Neil Warnock 2012 - 2013
Don Revie 1961 - 1974	Brian McDermott 2013 - 2014
Brian Clough 1974	David Hockaday 2014 (June - August)
Jimmy Armfield 1974 - 1978	Darko Milanič 2014 (September - October)
Jock Stein 1978 (Aug - Sept)	Neil Redfearn 2014 - 2015
Jimmy Adamson 1978 - 1980	Uwe Rosler 2015 (May - October)
Allan Clarke 1980 - 1982	Steve Evans 2015 – 2016
Eddie Gray 1982 - 1985	Garry Monk 2016 – 2017
Billy Bremner 1985 - 1988	Thomas Christiansen 2017 – 2018
Howard Wilkinson 1988 - 1996	Paul Heckingbottom 2018 (February – June)
George Graham 1996 - 1998	Marcelo Bielsa 2018 - Present

QUIZ ANSWERS

THE BIG LEEDS UNITED QUIZ p40-41

1. Kemar Roofe
2. Middlesbrough
3. Pablo Hernandez
4. 23
5. West Bromwich Albion
6. Goalkeeper
7. Chelsea
8. 4
9. Don Revie
10. 15
11. Forest Green Rovers
12. Spanish
13. Ezgjan Alioski
14. Burton Albion
15. 19
16. Once
17. 24
18. Bristol City
19. Polish
20. 1992

SPOT THE DIFFERENCE p45

PLAYER FACTS p43

Joined Leeds United from Wolverhampton Wanderers in July 2018 = Barry Douglas

Wears shirt number 28 for Leeds United = Gaetano Berardi

Played for Sweden at the 2018 FIFA World Cup = Pontus Jansson

Played in the MLS for New York City and is on loan at Leeds United from Manchester City = Jack Harrison

Is the captain of Leeds United and wears squad number 6 = Liam Cooper

GOING FOR GOAL (MAZE) p49

QUIZ ANSWERS

SPOT THE BALL p53

CROSSWORD p55

PABLOHERNANDEZ
EDDIEGRAY SWANSEA BILLYBREMNER
LUCAS
WHITE LUCASRADEBE STOKECITY
BLUE ARGENTINA
NORTHERNIRELAND

WORDSEARCH p57

WHERE'S LUCAS

Can you spot Lucas within the crowd of Leeds United supporters at Elland Road?